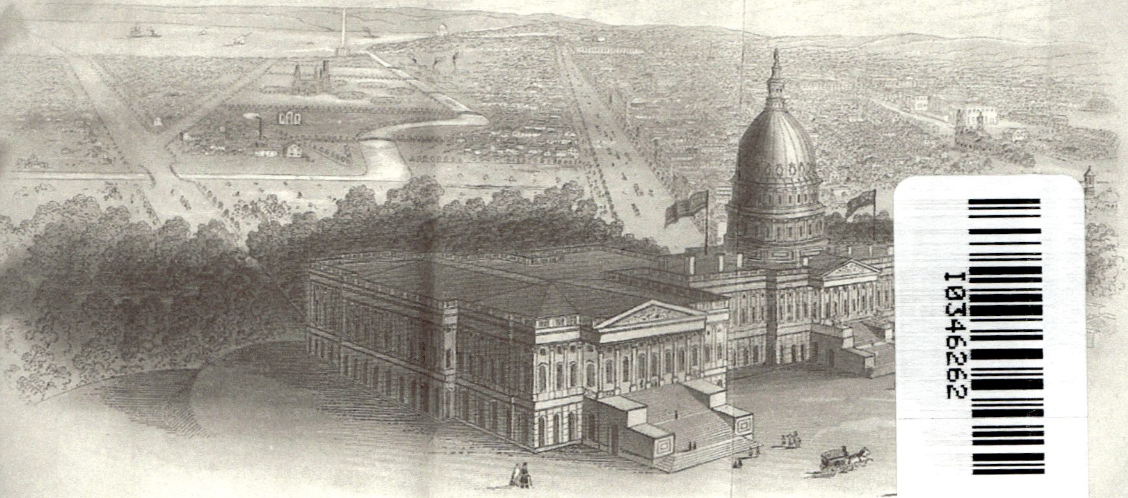

View of Washington City —— Pub by W.H. & O.H. Morrison

MORRISONS'
STRANGER'S GUIDE

AND

ETIQUETTE,

FOR

WASHINGTON CITY

AND

ITS VICINITY.

ILLUSTRATED WITH WOOD AND STEEL ENGRAVINGS, ENTIRELY RE-WRITTEN AND BROUGHT DOWN TO THE PRESENT TIME.

WASHINGTON:
W. H. & O. H. MORRISON.
1862.

Entered according to the act of Congress, in the year 1859, by W. H. & O. H. MORRISON, in the clerk's office of the District Court for the District of Columbia.

M'GILL & WITHEROW, PRINTERS, PENNSYLVANIA AVENUE, NEAR ELEVENTH STREET.

CONTENTS.

STRANGER'S GUIDE.

Washington	7
The Capitol	9
The Patent Office	21
The Post Office Department	22
Treasury Department	23
The President's House	25
The Smithsonian Institution	27
The Navy Yard	30
The National Observatory	30
The City Hall	31
The Congressional Burying Ground	32
Washington Monument	33
Discovery of America	35
Civilization	36
Statue of Washington	36
Jackson Monument	36
Georgetown	38
Bladensburg	38
Alexandria	38
The Potomac at the Little Falls	39
Hospital for the Insane	39
Military Asylum	40
Mills' Statue of Washington	42
The National Armory	43
Mount Vernon	44

ETIQUTTE OF WASHINGTON.

Introductory Remarks	47
Cleanliness	50
Dress	51
Introductions, Cards, Visiting, &c.	52
Evening Parties	55
Dinners	56
Deportment in the Street	59
Balls	60
Visits to Official Persons on Business	61
The President	61

NOTICE.

We present to the public the fifth edition of this little work; or we should more properly say, a new work, embracing a Guide to Washington, with the more essential rules of polite society in the Metropolis. It has been entirely rewritten, and embraces a description of all the public buildings, grounds, and objects of interest in the city and its vicinity.

It is believed that no work of the kind embraces a greater amount of valuable information for strangers and citizens in so short a compass.

Stranger's Guide.

WASHINGTON CITY.

Washington, the Seat of Government of the United States, is situated at the head of tide-water and of navigation on the Potomac, the broadest, and, in many respects, the most beautiful river in the Union. The city is surrounded by hills on the east, north, and west, forming an amphitheatre, from the sides and tops of which every house and street is visible.

The engraving presents a view of the city, with the Capitol in the foreground. On the right are seen the towers of Trinity Church, the City Hall, the Post Office, and Patent Office, and far beyond is the lofty range of hills above Georgetown. Pennsylvania Avenue, with its beautiful rows of trees, and its busy throngs, is seen in the centre; to the left of it the meandering course of the Washington Canal is marked by a white line; and on the extreme left is Maryland Avenue, leading to the Potomac, which is in full view. Immediately west of the Capitol, and between the two Avenues, are the Columbian Armory, the Smithsonian Institution, and the Washington Monument. The hills beyond the river are in Alexandria county, Virginia.

No city in the Union, perhaps, has a more beautiful site than Washington, and few are better situated for manufactures and commerce. But, with Baltimore and Alexandria in the immediate vicinity, which had many years the start of it, Washington may be said to have literally no commerce, and her manufacturing enterprises are yet in their infancy. The Federal Government, with its annual distribution of official prizes, has hitherto monopolized the attention of a majority of those who have turned their ambitious thoughts towards the Seat of Government; and the great natural advantages of the position for business enterprises have been neglected. The city is cotemporaneous with the Capitol. Prior to the location of the Seat of Government at this place, there was not even a village where Washington now stands. The act bears date July 16th, 1790; and, as may be supposed, population immediately began to flow to it, though less rapidly than was anticipated. The number of inhabitants is at present supposed to be near seventy thousand. The magnitude of the plan of the city, and the distances of the public edifices from each other, seem to have retarded its growth, as the responsibility of paving the immense streets, with one exception, has been thrown upon the city. But these early difficulties are now overcome, and Washington is rapidly rising into importance as a city. Within ten years the style of private building has greatly improved, and become more worthy of the noble public edifices in their midst. The munificent supply of water by a grand Aqueduct, which, while it is a tardy fulfillment of the original plan of the city, will add greatly to the prosperity of the place, as well as to its beauty, interest, and comfort.

Public Buildings, etc.

THE CAPITOL.

The Capitol has a noble and commanding situation upon the brow of a hill, a mile northeast of the Potomac. From its roof the eye surveys a magnificent panorama of the surrounding country. The river is seen to emerge from the narrow gorges of the hills in the direction of the Blue Ridge. Suddenly it turns from a nearly eastern to a southern direction, and meeting with the ocean tides, it widens into a bay a mile in width, whose placid waters mirror the elevated slopes which wall it in on either side. The site is worthy of the noble structure which stands upon it.

The Capitol, like Rome, was not built in a day. It has gradually grown up with the country, but, like the country, it was modeled upon a great scale, and with an eye to future enlargements. The corner-stone of the old building, which now constitutes the centre of the new edifice, was laid on the 18th September, 1793, by General Washington, in the presence of a large concourse of citizens, and with imposing ceremonials. The plan was drawn by Dr. Thornton, and the work executed under several successive architects, (Messrs. Hallet, Hadfield, Hoban, and Latrobe,) but was not complete when it was destroyed by the British army in 1814. It was rebuilt in the course of the succeeding ten years; but after a quarter of a century it was found inadequate in many respects to the public convenience. It is 352 feet 4 inches in length. The width of the wings is 121 feet, and the width of the centre, including the portico and steps, 290 feet. This whole structure, including centre and wings, becomes the centre of the new building. The corner-stone of the new wings was laid by President Fillmore on the 4th of July, 1851. Mr. Webster delivered an oration on the occasion. They are connected with the main building by corridors, each 44 feet in length and 56 in width. The wings are each 324 feet in length, from east to west, including porticos and steps, by 152 feet 8 inches from north to south, including porticos. The total length of the whole edifice is made up of the old centre building, the corridors, and the width of the two new wings. It is therefore 745 feet 8 inches.

The material of the old edifice is yellow sandstone, which has been painted white, to beautify and preserve it. The wings are of white marble. The architecture is Corinthian, and the style of finish, exterior and interior, is elaborate. We have no room for a general description. The new dome, as presented in the engraving, will rise 241 feet above the top of the building, and 396 feet 4 inches above the level of the grounds at the foot of the terrace, or only 4 feet less than St. Paul's, and 36 feet less than St. Peter's. The material of the dome is cast-iron.

The Rotunda, though shorn of its glories while the new dome is being constructed, is still worthy of the especial attention of visitors. It is 96 feet in diameter, and its walls are ornamented with historical paintings and sculptures. Of the eight large paintings which occupy the panels in the lower surface of the walls, the four illustrative of revolutionary events are by Col. Trumbull, of Connecticut, who was an aid-de-camp of General Washington. They are greatly admired by the lovers of art. The events chosen by the artist for representation are, the Declaration of Independence, the Surrender of

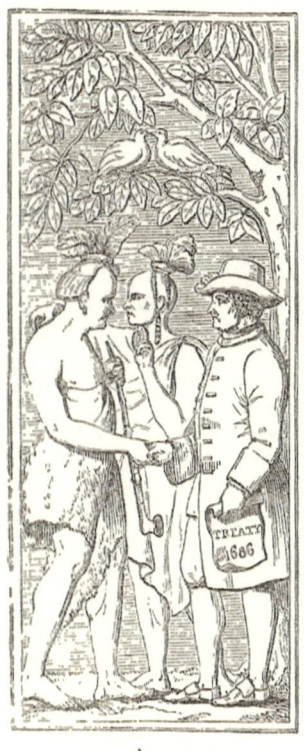

PENN'S TREATY.

BOONE & INDIANS.

General Burgoyne, at Saratoga, the Surrender of Cornwallis, at Yorktown, and the Resignation of the command of the Army by General Washington to Congress, at Annapolis, at the conclusion of peace. The other paintings in the opposite panels are, respectively, the Embarkation of the Pilgrims by Wier, the Landing of Columbus by Vanderlyn, De Soto's Discovery of the Mississippi by Powell, and the Baptism of Pocahontas by Chapman. These great paintings are all by American artists.

Above the four entrances to the Rotunda are four groups of sculpture in high relief, also illustrative of events in the history of the country. They are accurately delineated by our engravings. That over the north door represents Wm. Penn in the act of making a treaty with the Indians, under the shadow of an elm tree. On the opposite wall, Daniel Boone, the Pioneer of Kentucky, is represented in a desperate hand to hand conflict with Indians. This group speaks for itself, and needs no description A band of Winnebago Indians who visited Washington some years ago, were greatly affected by it, and actually raised the war-whoop in the Rotunda; when, perhaps frightened at the sound of their own voices echoed through the lofty dome, they fled from the hall.

Over the eastern doorway is a group representing the landing of the Pilgrims at Plymouth Rock, Mass-

LANDING OF THE PILGRIMS.

CAPTAIN SMITH AND POCAHONTAS.

achusetts. The boat has just touched the rock, when the Englishman is met by the Indian with the offer of an ear of corn, as a symbol of hospitality and friendship. The child of the white man seems to beg his father not to venture on shore, while the mother looks with trustful eyes to heaven.

Over the western door Pocahontas is shown in the act of shielding Captain John Smith, the pioneer colonist of Virginia, from the savage ferocity of her father, Powhatan, by thrusting her form between him and his victim. These groups are by Italian and French artists, and are greatly admired.

Under the eastern portico, on the north side of the entrance to the Rotunda, is a statue of War, by Persico, an Italian. It is 9 feet high, of Carrara marble. There is nothing fierce or ferocious in this piece; the angry brow and the determined bearing are rather expressive of indignation at wrong, and a conscious power to punish it.

On the opposite side of the door, Peace is personified by a maiden, who, in simple garb, and with the expression of the sweetness of woman, extends the olive branch to her warlike brother. These pieces are highly finished.

The interior architecture of the extension is elaborately finished. The walls are decorated with fresco paintings, and the floors are covered with encaustic tiling. The walls of the Vice Presi-

WAR.

PEACE.

dent's room are entirely of Tennessee and Italian marble. There is also a retiring room adjacent to the Senate chamber, whose walls and ceilings are richly covered with gilt.

The new Senate Chamber and House of Representatives are worthy of the especial attention of strangers. They are entirely similar in construction, but differ in size and finish. They are situated in the centres respectively of the north and south wings of the Capitol, with continuous Halls running around them, and separating them from the outer walls, or from the committee rooms. They are therefore necessarily lighted from above. The ceilings are cast-iron frame works, the large square panels being filled with glass richly embellished with symbolic representations of the arts, history, and characteristics of the country. These rich ceilings temper while they admit the light of day which comes without stint through the glass roofs above. There is also an arrangement of movable metallic plates, on the principle of Venitian blinds, under the sunny sides of the respective roofs; so that when the sun is at meridian height, and when it is descending in the west, the amount of light admitted may be the same. Above the ceiling there is an ingenious and complicated apparatus for lighting the Halls with gas, the effect of which is to produce a light scarcely distinguishable from that of day. The ventilation of these Halls is admirable.

The Senate Chamber is 113 feet 3 inches long, by 80 feet 3 inches wide. These dimensions include the galleries, which extend entirely around, and will accommodate about one thousand persons. The space under the galleries is partitioned off into small apartments, and the area of the floor is diminished to that extent. It is 83 feet 11 inches long by 51 feet 1 inch wide.

The House of Representatives is 139 feet long by 93 feet wide, in its greatest extent. The floor is 113 feet by 67. The galleries will accommodate some fifteen hundred persons. The elevation of either Hall is 37 feet. The accurate pictures which accompany these descriptions will render them perfectly intelligible to every reader.

The grounds surrounding the Capitol, which now embrace about thirty acres, and which are famed for their beauty, are to be enlarged to some four or five times their present dimensions. The whole cost of the Capitol, including the old and new additions, with the ground that surrounds it, will amount to perhaps ten or twelve millions of dollars. T. U. Walter, Esq., is the architect of the extension and the dome. The work has been under the superintendence of Captain M. C. Meigs, of the Engineer Corps.

THE PATENT OFFICE.

The Patent Office is sometimes miscalled the Interior Department, because the Secretary of the Department with his clerks occupy it, as a matter of temporary convenience. But it was built for a Patent Office simply; and at the rate of increase of the business of that bureau, a very few years will suffice to fill the building with what pertains to patents, to the exclusion of everything else. It occupies two whole squares, and fronts south on F street, north on G street, east on Seventh street, and west on Ninth street. The length of the building from Seventh to Ninth street is 410 feet, and the width from F to G is 275 feet. The inner quadrangle is about 265 feet by 135. The style of architecture is Doric, and although the finish is exceedingly plain, no building in Washington is more admired than the Patent Office. The grand but simple majesty of its proportions seems to address the sense of beauty in the least as well as in the most cultivated minds.

The interior is marked by the same combination of plainness of decoration with grandeur of design. The lower stories are divided into apartments suitable for the business of the office, while the upper or third story forms one grand saloon, running entirely around the quadrangle, measuring 1350 feet in length in its outer surface. This room is occupied by the models of the patents, admirably arranged on either side upon shelves, while ample space is left in the centre for promenading around the entire quadrangle.

There are porticos on the east, west, and south. The latter is an exact copy of the portico of the Pantheon at Rome. The eastern portico is greatly admired. The centre of the south front of the Patent Office was built of inferior brown sandstone, and is painted to correspond with the beautiful crystallized marble of the other portions of the building. Wm. P. Elliott was the original designer of this edifice, but it has been built under other architects.

THE POST OFFICE DEPARTMENT.

The Post Office Department, like the Patent Office and Treasury, has been greatly enlarged within a few years. The first building erected for the accommodation of the Department was burnt on the 15th December, 1836; and the foundation of the present edifice, which was designed by Robert Mills, was laid in the summer of 1839. The extension, designed by Mr. Walter, was commenced in June, 1855. The design is carried out in conformity with the original building, though greatly modified and improved in its architectual details and embellishments. Captain Meigs has superintended the work. The style is what is called Palatial, and the order a modified Corinthian. The columns of the extension are monoliths of Italian marble. The whole structure is marble, but the old part is inferior to the new, both in material and finish. It covers an entire square, and is bounded by Seventh and Eighth streets on the east and west, and F and E on the north and south.

The length of the building from north to south is 300 feet, and the width from east to west is 204 feet. The interior is divided into small apartments for business purposes. Visitors should inquire for the book of post office accounts kept by Dr. Franklin, the first Postmaster General for the Colonies; also for the Dead Letter Office. The City Post Office occupies the lower story of the north front, and is well arranged.

TREASURY DEPARTMENT.

The old portion of the Treasury Department fronts on Fifteenth street, between Pennsylvania avenue and G street. It stands on the site of the old Treasury building, (which was burnt in the spring of 1833.) It was commenced in the summer of 1836, and presented an unbroken Ionic colonnade 342 feet long, with the ends unfinished. The extension, the foundation of which was laid in September, 1855, designed by Mr. Walter, and superintended by Mr. Young, who has designed many important details, is a great improvement on the old structure. The design, the materials used, and the execution are all superior. The old building is of inferior brown sandstone painted; and the colonnade, though imposing in appearance, is monotonous and inconvenient, as it serves to exclude the light from the building. The extension flanks the old building at each end with massive and beautiful terminations of the north and south fronts, which break the monotony of the long portico of the original building. There are two inner quadrangles, formed by the old rear building, extending back from the eastern entrance. These courts are each 130 feet square. The walls of the extension are composed of pilasters, resting on a base which rises some twelve feet above the ground on the southern or lower side. Between the pilasters or antæ are fillings tastefully arranged so as to form door and window facings with beautiful mouldings. In the centre of the southern, western, and northern fronts are magnificent porticos in the Ionic order. The west front has also the projecting pediments at the ends, corresponding with those on the east side, and each supported by square antæ at the angles, with the two columns between. The whole new structure is of the best and most beautiful granite in the world, brought from Dix island, on the coast of Maine. The antæ and columns are monoliths. The large solid antæ weigh nearly an hundred thousand pounds, and the columns some seventy-five thousand. The facility with which these immense masses are hewn out of the quarries, swung on board vessels, brought to the Capitol, and raised to the positions which the architect in his studio designed them to occupy, conveys a high idea of American art and enterprise. The Treasury Department, as extended, will be 465 feet long, exclusive of the porticos, by 266 feet wide. The interior arrangements are admirable; and the interior architectural ornamentation, while it is more elaborate than in other public buildings except the Capitol, is peculiarly American in its details. The composite capitals of the interior, as well as the moulding, are worthy of especial attention.

THE PRESIDENT'S HOUSE.

The President's House is situated upon the highest ground, and nearly midway between the Capitol and Georgetown, one mile and a half from the former. It has a fine view down the Potomac, with Alexandria and Fort Washington in full view. The grounds about the President's House are tastefully adorned with artificial mounds, gravel-walks, trees, and a fountain. The house has a rustic base, which on the south side is entirely above ground, and gives a facade of three stories. On the north, but two stories rise above the level. The main building is 170 feet long by 86 feet deep. It is of sand-stone painted white, with Ionic pilasters. The building is cotemporary in age with the Capitol. While General Jackson was President, a portico was added on the north side. The south side has a bow in the centre, with a portico of corresponding shape. Appended to the main building, at either end, are long, low ranges of stalls with flat roofs, which are used for various household purposes. That on the west is surmounted by a beautiful green-house, which is filled with exotic plants. The public approach the President's House on the north side, except on Wednesday evenings in summer, when a sort of out-door reception is given, accompanied with music, in the grounds on the south side. The entrance from the north porch is into a long vestibule, through which the visitor passes to the right into the President's reception room. This communicates with the Round room, formed by the south bow front, and this with a Square room, which adjoins the great East room. This last is the grand parlor of the President. As its name indicates, it is in the east end of the building, and extends entirely across the house from north to south. It is 80 feet long by 40 wide, and 22 high. These rooms are elegantly but not extravagantly finished and furnished. They can be seen at all times by strangers—the President only at certain hours set apart by himself.

THE SMITHSONIAN INSTITUTION.

James Smithson, an English gentleman of liberal education, died at Genoa, in the year 1828, leaving his property to an only son, and in the event of the death of that son without heirs, to the United States, "to found at Washington, under the name of the Smithsonian Institution, an establishment for the increase and diffusion of knowledge among men." According to the expectation of the testator, the heir of Mr. Smithson, who was in an almost hopeless state of consumption, died without heirs, and the property, valued at half a million of dollars, reverted to the United States. Congress accepted the bequest on the 1st day of July, 1836, and the fund was received into the Treasury, September 1st, 1838. After a prolonged discussion a law was passed in 1846, for the establishment of the Institution as it now exists. The building was erected about twelve years ago of red sandstone. It is situated in an open space between the Capitol and the Washington Monument, and is surrounded by an enclosure extending from Seventh to Twelfth street, and from the canal to B street south. The area enclosed contains about fifty acres, and the greater part of it was beautifully improved under the direction of the late Mr. Downing. The building was planned by Mr. Renwick in Romanesque style. It consists of a centre building 250 feet long and 55 feet broad; two connecting ranges or cloisters, 60 feet each; and two wings, each 40 feet by 80. The entire length of the building is therefore 450 feet. The north entrance passes under a double tower; the one on the right hand, which is octagonal, being 145 feet high. The south entrance passes under a large but not very elevated square tower. The main building is also flanked at each angle by a tower; and the wings have smaller towers. The towers contain the stairways. The whole lower story of the centre building is in one grand apartment, 250 feet long by 50 in width, occupied by the museum. The Library is in the west wing. The east wing is occupied by the family of the Secretary or Superintendent of the Institution. The Lecture Room, capable of seating fifteen hundred people, is in the centre of the main building on the second floor. On the east of it is a large room containing the chemical and philosophical apparatus; and on the west is a room of corresponding dimensions, at present used as a picture gallery. The Museum now contains the articles brought by the Exploring Expedition, which for many years were deposited in the Patent Office. The visitor will be interested to observe, that while the Smithsonian is a regular building, with a centre united to wings by cloisters, yet there are no two parts alike. There are no two towers or facades alike. This is an interesting feature of the Institution, and pleases by its variety, while it satisfies the love of symmetry by the regular correspondence of the parts. Free lectures on science and literature are given three times a week during the winter; and throughout the year visitors are admitted between the hours of 9 a. m. and 5 p. m. The Library is for the most part composed of works of science, a large portion of them being in foreign languages. The Museum embraces the articles which for many years were desposited at the Patent Office, with other interesting collections. In the department of natural history are extensive collections of the reptile races, preserved in alcohol, together with a great variety of skins of American animals, which are being stuffed for exhibition. The Picture Gallery contains Stanley's numerous collection of Indian portraits, taken from life by the artist, who spent several years among the Indians in Oregon, California, and the western Territories. The gallery also contains the Dying Gladiator.

THE NAVY YARD.

The Washington Navy Yard is situated near the mouth of the East Branch of the Potomac, one mile southeast of the Capitol. This yard, though less extensive than those of Brooklyn, Gosport, and Boston, is a place of much interest to strangers. It contains two ship-houses, and a great number of machine shops, in which whatever pertains to the naval service is manufactured. The grounds, embracing some 25 acres, are tastefully improved. They are open to visitors throughout every day, except Sunday.

THE NATIONAL OBSERVATORY.

This institution, which is destined to play a distinguished part in the world of science, has already, though founded in 1842, acquired a European reputation, by the important discoveries made by Lieut. Maury, of the Navy, who almost from its origin has had charge of it. It is admirably located on a high knob, near the Potomac, between the President's House and Georgetown. It is supplied with a superior telescope and other apparatus for observing the heavens and the phenomena of the atmosphere, a description of which our limits will not permit.

Strangers can visit it at all hours, and are permitted to inspect the telescope and other istruments when they are not in use. Telegraph wires connect this observatory with all others in the Union, so that simultaneous observations of the heavenly bodies and the conditions of the atmosphere may be made and compared.

THE CITY HALL.

The City Hall has never been finished according to the design of George Hadfield. It was begun in 1820. About a dozen years ago the south, east, and west fronts were stuccoed, and a portico added, in the Ionic order. The length is 200 feet, but it is too shallow, and contains no apartment of suitable dimensions for court rooms. Its appearance is imposing. It is situated at the head of Four-and-a Half street, at the junction of Louisiana avenue and Indiana avenue with D street. The Circuit and Criminal Courts of the District of Columbia are held here, together with the Mayor's and other offices connected with the city government.

THE CONGRESSIONAL BURYING GROUND.

This Cemetery is generally supposed to be the property of the Federal Government, and to have been especially designated as a burial place for Members of Congress and other distinguished official personages. This, however, is a mistake, originating in the name assumed for it. It is the property of one of the Episcopal churches, and the Government is in no way responsible for its preservation.

This venerable city of the dead has partaken of the general prosperity of the community, and has recently enlarged its borders by the addition of several acres. It now embraces nearly twenty acres. It contains a plain cenotaph for each member of Congress who has died during the term for which he was elected, since the Capitol has been located in Washington. There are several monuments of interest. Among these is one erected to George Clinton, also one to Elbridge Gerry, and one to William Wirt. In the plain old vault near the centre of the grounds, the remains of General Taylor and Mr. Calhoun reposed for several days. The Congressional Burying Ground is beautifully situated on the banks of the East Branch, about a mile above the Navy Yard, with the noble range of forest-clad hills on the opposite side of the beautiful expanse of water, forever looking down upon the peaceful repose of the dead.

WASHINGTON MONUMENT.

The design of the Washington Monument contemplates a shaft 600 feet in height. The marble obelisk, resting on a foundation of gneiss $17\frac{1}{2}$ feet high, is 55 feet square at the base. This foundation is 81 feet square, and extends eight feet below the surface. The wall of the obelisk is 15 feet thick at the base, and gradually tapers on the outside. The inside of the wall is perpendicular, and the enclosed space is 25 feet square. The fifteen foot wall will ascend until the gentle taper reduces it to two feet in thickness. The interior walls will be ornamented by the insertion of the numerous specimen pieces sent from all parts of the world as tributes to the memory of Washington. They are so arranged as not to be covered by the stairway, which will ascend to the top of the Monument.

The pantheon base, as represented in engravings, was a part of the plan originally selected, but it is now highly probable that it will be dispensed with, and that the plain square base, which is characteristic of the obelisk, will be substituted. This change in the plan, while it will reduce the cost of the Monument to one-half the sum contemplated in connection with the pantheon, will, at the same time, conform it to the recognized rules of art. There is now reason to hope that the Monument, under its new auspices, will be completed in a few years. It will be the highest structure in the world, and yet it will form only a well-deserved tribute to the man whom Lord Brougham has announced "the greatest ruler of any age."

The Monument is now 170 feet high, and has cost thus far $230,000. The total cost of the obelisk has been estimated at $552,000. The pantheon was estimated to cost $570,000 alone; but a plain and appropriate base may be built for less than a tenth of that sum. The visitor to Washington should not fail to examine the interesting contributions of ornamented blocks of marble and stone from all parts of the world. Such of them as have not been inserted in the wall, too high for inspection at present, can be seen in a shed near the Monument.

Some of the most celebrated obelisks in the world, if compared with this, dwindle into insignificance. As, for instance:

Antonine's Column, at Rome, is	135 ft.
Trajan's Column " "	145
Principal Tower of Smithsonian	145
Napoleon's Column, Paris	150
Washington Column, Baltimore	181
Sesostris' Obelisk, Thebes	200
Bunker Hill Monument, Boston	220
Column of Delhi	262
St. Paul's, London	320

Cathedral Tower, Strasburg................460 ft.
St. Peter's, Rome................................465
Great Pyramid of Cheops, Egypt...........480
Tower of Malines, Belgium...................550
Washington Monument, Washington......600

DISCOVERY OF AMERICA.

This group occupies the southern abutment of the steps leading into the portico of the Capitol. It is by Persico. It represents Columbus landed in America. He holds a globe in his right hand, symbolic of his discovery of a new world. He is encased in armor, and the artist is said to have copied it, to a rivet, from a suit worn by Columbus. The figure on his right is an Indian female, and her attitude expresses the astonishment and dismay which was manifested by her race on first beholding Europeans.

CIVILIZATION.

This group by Greenough represents the conflict of civilization with savage life. The female figure on the left represents a terror-stricken mother holding her child, while the murderous savage is arrested by the father, as his arm is raised to deal the deadly blow. The dog on the right looks on the conflict with eager interest. This group has been greatly admired by the lovers of art.

STATUE OF WASHINGTON.

Greenough's Statue of Washington, of colossal size, sits on a pedestal of granite, in the grounds east of the Capitol. The Father of his Country is represented in a sitting posture, with his right hand pointed to heaven, while the left holds a Roman sword, with the handle turned from the person, symbolic of his trust in Providence, and ascription of the glory of his achievements to that source. The statue is of one piece of marble, though not pure white. It is greatly admired by persons whose tastes have been cultivated and familiarized with works of art. Mr. Everett regards it as one of the greatest works of sculpture of modern times.

JACKSON MONUMENT.

The Jackson Monument stands in the centre of Lafayette square, opposite the President's House.

It is a bronze equestrian statue, by Clark Mills. The noble steed stands poised upon the hind feet, the first and perhaps the only instance of the kind in the world. Mr. Mills, by consulting nature, ascertained the true position of the several parts of the body of the horse in the act of rearing, and thus overcame the apparently insurmountable obstacles in the way. The animal naturally throws himself back on his haunches until the feet reach the centre of gravity. The artist has simply copied nature, and it is a great mistake to suppose that the statue is held in place by the rivets which attach the feet to the pedestal; they would be entirely inadequate to such a strain. These rivets are doubtless a useful provision against accidents, but they are not essential in keeping the horse poised, even during a violent wind. Mr. Mills exhibits a small model, which satisfactorily illustrates this principle. The statue is composed of cannon taken by General Jackson in his battles with the English. The likeness is deemed good. The General is represented in the act of waiving his hand in acknowledgment of honors paid him while reviewing his troops. This monument to the hero of New Orleans was erected on the 8th of January, 1853, the anniversary of the battle, on which occasion Mr. Douglas delivered an appropriate oration.

GEORGETOWN.

This old place is separated from Washington by Rock creek, which is a mile northwest of the President's House. The scenery in this vicinity is well worth the attention of strangers. The town has near ten thousand inhabitants, and is coterminous with Washington on the west.

BLADENSBURG.

Bladensburg is noted for the duelling-ground in its vicinity, which is a ravine three-quarters of a mile from the town, in the direction of Washington. Bladensburg was also the scene of a not very creditable battle with the British forces in 1814, if, indeed the complete rout and dispersion of the American militia can be called a battle. The town is five miles northeast of the Capitol.

ALEXANDRIA.

This town is situated about six miles below Washington, and in full view. It belonged to the District of Columbia from 1790 to 1846, when it, as a part of the county of the same name, in which it is situated, was retroceded to Virginia. It now has some fifteen thousand inhabitants, and is improving. It has a high, healthy, and beautiful situation, with a fine harbor.

THE POTOMAC AT THE LITTLE FALLS.

The Potomac, below the Little Falls, rushes through the narrow space between the two piers of the bridge, with the high range of hills in the background, rising abruptly and almost perpendicularly from the water. The scene is wild and interesting. It is only four miles above Washington. Immediately below this bridge, the narrow mountain stream meets the tides from the ocean, and four miles below it presents an expanse of water a mile in width. The scene is wild and romantic.

HOSPITAL FOR THE INSANE.

The Hospital for the Insane of the Army and Navy and District of Columbia occupies a noble site on the east bank of the Potomac, near its confluence with the East Branch. The eminence on which it stands is one of the highest in the vicinity of the Capital, and commands the finest view of the city anywhere to be had. The edifice is an immense structure, 711 feet in length. It is in the collegiate style of Gothic architecture, and is divided into sections, receding on either hand from the centre building and from each other, thus giving corridors in each section for the admission of the light. This idea, says the architect, Mr. Walter, was suggested by Dr. Nichols, the superintendent. The centre building is enriched by buttresses on the corners, and a magnificent oriel window ornaments the main tower. The windows are finished with hood mouldings formed of cast-iron. The whole is surmounted by embattled parapets, and presents a facade of great richness, notwithstanding extreme simplicity of detail. The material of the building is brick on a foundation of gneiss. The interior is subdivided into various suites of apartments adapted to the condition of the patients. The hospital is open to visitors on Wednesday. The number of inmates at present is about 120.

THE MILITARY ASYLUM.

This building occupies a high plateau about three miles north of the Capitol, which for beauty and salubrity is unsurpassed; but its greatest charm is the noble view down the Potomac river, with the city in the foreground. From no other point about Washington, perhaps, does the river scenery appear to equal advantage. The noble range of hills which enclose the river are seen stretching away down to the vicinity of Mount Vernon, where the sudden bend in the stream cuts short the view, and gives the appearance of a lake walled in by mountains. The Asylum is in the Norman style, of East Chester marble, roughly dressed or "pointed." It is 593 feet in length, by 58 ft. 4 in. in breadth, with a rear building, called the mess-room, 60 feet in length. Projecting from the centre of the south, or front, is a tower 82 feet high above the surface of the ground. From the top of this tower the eye can survey a distance of country twenty-five or thirty miles in diameter. The edifice is divided into 42 rooms, exclusive of the cellar.

Near the main structure are two small buildings in cottage style, designated as officers' quarters Nos. 1 and 2. The first is 52 ft. by 40, and surrounded by a piazza. No. 2 is 48 by 40, and in the same style. The President has for two summers past occupied these quarters with his family.

MILLS' STATUE OF WASHINGTON.

In 1853, Congress appropriated $50,000 for the erection, by Clark Mills, Esq., of an equestrian statue of Washington. In compliance with this order, Mr. Mills has chosen for illustration the courage and daring by which Washington, at the crisis of the battle of Princeton, rallied his troops, and turned the scale in favor of his country's cause, by what, at another time, would have been a reckless exposure of his person. The incident is familiar to the student of history. The horse is represented as shrinking back before the destructive fire of the enemy, while his rider surveys the scene with the calmness and resolution which know no fear, when honor and duty are at stake. The head and face of Washington are from a bust by Houdon, taken in Washington's lifetime, and which remained at Mount Vernon. The likeness is, doubtless, one of the best in existence. The statue is collossal in size, being eleven feet, if standing erect, and upon horseback, fifteen feet.

The original design contemplated only a plain pedestal like that of the Jackson Statue in Lafayette square ; but Mr. Mills has sketched a pedestal, which, while it will symbolize the history of the country from the earliest times, will be in harmony with the main design. The proposed pedestal has four concave faces, each of which is divided into three tiers, one above the other, and these again are subdivided into sections. The lower tier begins with the aboriginal period, when this great continent was known only to wild savages. In a succession of low reliefs, the Indian is seen in pursuit of the buffalo, the bear, elk, moose, and other animals; also the wars and war dances of the savages are represented. The second tier, in higher relief, illustrates the discovery of America by Europeans; their landing, first permanent settlements, their struggles with the savages, and their final triumph; also their early struggles with the mother country—the tea is thrown overboard at Boston, and the declaration of independence is represented. The third tier, in full relief, represents the events of the Revolution, with all the more distinguished officers. The proposed grand historical pedestal will be fitly surmounted by the collossal equestrian statue of the Father of his Country.

THE NATIONAL ARMORY.

This building is situated on the public ground between the Smithsonian Institute and the Capitol. The design has not yet been completed. Only the centre has been erected, which is 103 feet in length, by 57 in width. It is three stories high. The floors of the second and third stories are supported upon iron columns. When completed, it will present a fine appearance. It is designed as a depository of arms for the volunteer militia of the District of Columbia, as well as of national trophies, relics, flags, &c. The latter circumstance will give to it a national importance, and make it well worthy the attention of strangers.

MOUNT VERNON.

Mount Vernon (not the house, but the place) is worthy to have been the residence of Washington. A more noble and commanding view of the river scenery is scarcely anywhere to be seen. The house is of wood, two stories high, and ninety-six feet long, and surmounted by a cupola. In the time of Washington it presented a fine appearance. It is now in a state of dilapidation, and is only an object of interest from association with a great name, and from the remarkable beauty of its surroundings. Mount Vernon is fifteen miles below Washington, on the Virginia side of the Potomac. It is usually visited in steamboats, which run twice a week from Washington. The Mausoleum is of plain brick. The white marble sarcophagi of General and Mrs. Washington can be seen through the iron bars which close up the gate or doorway. The Mount Vernon house and grounds, including the Tomb, have now passed into the hands of the "Mount Vernon Association," and it is hoped that a mausoleum worthy of the Father of his Country will be erected over his remains.

Etiquette of Washington.

INTRODUCTORY REMARKS.

It is not so much our object in this little volume to present a dissertation upon the laws of polite society in general, as to supply strangers with the more important conventional rules which regulate social and official intercourse at the Seat of Government. We shall therefore omit many things which properly find a place in books treating of Etiquette.

Good-breeding is a phrase of English origin, and literally implies ancient descent, or aristocratic lineage, as well as good manners. It is a figurative expression. It assumes that high birth necessarily implies politeness and refinement; but the common sense of mankind has come to regard the thing signified as the essential, and the figure is forgotten or disregarded. This is especially true in America, where the sentiment of Burns that

"Rank is but the guinea's stamp,"

has perhaps a more practical acceptance than in any other portion of the world. In this age, however, even in Europe, the character of the gentleman is measured, not by the extent of his paternal estate, or by the length of his pedigree, but by his moral and intellectual worth and good manners. Dr. Franklin, the son of a tallow-chandler, and a printer by profession, was regarded at the French court as a model of good-breeding. The dignity and suavity of his deportment, and the charm of his conversation, which was free alike from pedantry, dogmatism, and arrogance, won all hearts.

The term good-breeding, therefore, as modified by custom and experience, simply implies good manners, or propriety of behavior. There can be no good-breeding without a basis of good principles. Honor, truth, and disinterestedness, are the essential foundations of true politeness. But they are not all that is necessary to constitute that social virtue. Politeness implies elegance, refinement, polish, as well as just and liberal views. Indeed, so essential are these graces of education or habit to the character of the gentleman, that they are often mistaken for the more essential qualities; and we often hear the term gentleman applied to persons from whom the appellation of honest man would be withheld. On the other hand, we feel that in the true sense of the word, we could not justly apply the term gentleman to a person of rude, coarse, awkward, or slovenly manners, however honest and useful to society he might be.

Manners are everything to a lady or gentleman who expects to move in the best society. There must be perfect ease and self-possession, as well as freedom from arrogance and conceit. The gentleman will avoid party politics in mixed companies; and in Washington, where persons from all parts of the country and of the world are assembled, the injunction to avoid everything of a sectional nature is particularly appropriate. It argues a limited knowledge of the world, if not vulgarity and ignorance, to assume that all the company will receive your dogmatical assertions with favor; and, under any circumstances, a dictatorial and vociferous style of speech is vulgar and offensive to the last degree. If persons whose habit is to lay down the law in a peremptory and emphatic manner, accompanied by anathemas against all who doubt or question their infallibility, find they are becoming bores, they may well trace their misfortune to this fault. Let them learn to respect the opinions of others, and they may yet hope for forgiveness and restoration to society.

The impropriety of manners which proceeds from awkwardness, from thoughtlessness, or inexperience, may be overlooked; but when rudeness is the offspring of ill-nature, it ceases to be tolerable, and the offender should at once be shunned as an enemy to the peace, order, and happiness of society. People who delight in torturing the feelings of those with whom they are brought into association, and who only betray a recognition of the finer sensibilities of human nature by the ingenuity they display in pointing the arrows of malice and satire, are social outlaws. They have forfeited all claim to human sympathies, and should be sent to Coventry without appeal.

In the nature of things, it is impossible to give specific rules for behavior in the innumerable cases that may occur in the life of even one person. How idle, then, to think of giving such specific directions for society at large. In place, therefore, of an undertaking so utterly impracticable, we content ourselves with the general observations above, in which we have endeavored to suggest the true principles and motives which should control men and women in society, rather than to state rules.

But while it is impossible to give specific rules of behavior for all possible cases, it is not out of place, and may be highly useful to the young and inexperienced, to point out certain cardinal observances which are deemed prerequisites to admission into good society.

CLEANLINESS.

No man has a right to call himself a gentleman, or to claim the acquaintance of ladies, who is not scrupulously clean and neat. He may not be able to dress expensively, but he has no excuse for a want of cleanliness in a country abounding in pure fresh water. Gentlemen bathe the whole person frequently—a practice which is as conducive to health and long life as to respectability. It has been well said that cleanliness is akin to moral purity; and although we often meet with very depraved men who are neat in their persons, and very good men who are the reverse, the remark is not without its significance. The former may be said to "put on the livery of heaven to serve the devil in;" but we have no theory for explaining the folly of the latter. It is sad to see a man, otherwise entitled to respect and esteem, whose teeth are blackened with accumulations of tartar and tobacco juice, whose finger nails are tipped with ebony colored arcs, and whose hair and whiskers give countenance to the popular superstitions regarding witches and nightmares, which delight in spiriting away the victims of their persecutions through the key-hole, and tie knots in the hair for stirrups.

DRESS.

The very idea of a gentleman excludes that of a fop or dandy. A gentleman will dress well, but never gaudily. This rule alone, if properly attended

to, might serve for all that we have to say under
this head; but for the benefit of the young and inexperienced, whose welfare we have most at heart,
we will suggest a few things to be done, and others
to be omitted. We say, therefore, eschew an excess
of jewelry. A breast pin, or gold button, with a
chain, are very well. A ring is also worn by some.
Avoid gaudiness and singularity. Adapt your dress
to your complexion. Washington, though a small
place, is in one respect quite metropolitan. During
the winter its society is made up of materials gathered from all parts of the country, and all the styles as
well as all the politics of the country are represented here. A gentleman, therefore, may suit his taste
in respect to the shape and material of his hat, coat,
etc. The same remarks apply to the dress of ladies,
but they, in the nature of things, are allowed greater
variety of color, ornament, style, &c.

INTRODUCTION, CARDS, VISITING, &c.

It is not in good taste to give introductions, as a
matter of course, as is the custom in the country.
The reason of this restriction upon the natural dictates of polite and amiable natures can be best understood by those who live in cities. In the country,
where everybody knows everybody, and everybody's
business, the proverb that "a man is known

by the company he keeps," loses much of its significance; but in cities it is literally true, and hence the disinclination of city people to make acquaintances, whom it might become inconvenient or distasteful to recognize on all occasions.

It is safest, therefore, to omit introductions, without a previous understanding with the parties, even at the hazard of seeming rude. But common sense and a knowledge of the parties will teach any one the proper course to pursue.

The gentleman should always be presented to the lady, and an inferior in position to a superior. In each case the consent of the latter should be first obtained.

Letters of introduction should never be given unless the writer is well and favorably known to the person addressed, and he should be sure that the party introduced is worthy of respect and trust, in the capacity in which he is introduced. The latter may present the letter or not, as may suit his convenience. The letter should be left unsealed by the writer.

The bearer of a letter of introduction should send it with his card. He would thus avoid the awkwardness of waiting for a recognition while the party to whom it is addressed reads it. The latter may find it inconvenient to receive company, and the card would afford him an opportunity to decline.

But if the letter be on business, it should be presented in person. Business dispenses with ceremony. If you receive a letter introducing a gentleman, you should at least leave your card for him at his lodgings.

Cards are indispensable to the intercourse of polite society; but we are constrained by our limited space to omit specific directions for their use.

Visits of ceremony should be in the morning, and should not last more than five to twenty minutes. A card left at the door suffices for a morning call, among very fashionable people. It is to be borne in mind that, in the fashionable world, morning never breaks earlier than eleven o'clock, and usually lasts until three. The lady who receives calls should do so at once, or send a servant to excuse her. When the call is intended for both the lady and gentleman of the house, the name of the former only should be mentioned. In making a morning call, a gentleman should retain his hat in his hand, which the lady will not notice. But if a longer visit is intended, the hat, overcoat, &c., should be deposited in the hall before entering the room.

The lady of the house should never trouble her guests with her household derangements, nor the gentleman with his business. The topics selected for conversation should be general, and of an agreeable nature. If the company agree in politics or religion, it is delightful to interchange sentiments and impressions of passing events; but it is always awkward, if not disagreeable and rude, to introduce controverted questions. Very intelligent and polished people may discuss politics without offense, but it requires the utmost skill and delicacy to do so; and, as a general rule, all such discussions run into unpleasant disputation.

It is the custom in Washington for two or more ladies, during the day, to visit the Capitol, the Patent Office, the Smithsonian Institution, &c., unattended by gentlemen, as otherwise they might be debarred many enjoyments. Where it is inconvenient for a lady to find a female companion in such a walk, it is sufficient to have the attendance of a child.

EVENING PARTIES.

Evening parties are most appropriate to the winter. They are discontinued during Lent, but may be resumed afterwards. Cards of invitation should be sent to guests some days beforehand, and the latter should immediately accept, or decline with regret. The cards should be in the name of the lady, either written or engraved. Fashion has established nine o'clock as the hour at which the lady should be in her parlor to receive her guests; and from that hour to ten the guests are expected to arrive. The lady should have everything arranged so that she will not be compelled to leave her guests to superintend her household. The guests will be conducted to the dressing rooms, and the ladies having adjusted their toilets, will be attended to the drawing room by the gentlemen who accompany them. A servant sometimes announces the names of the guests as they enter the room. The lady will precede the gentleman or lean on his arm. The lady of the house will be near the door to receive them, and after a few words of greeting, they will pass on, and join in conversation with any of their acquaintances who may be present.

Gentlemen will not get together in groups, to the neglect of the ladies.

When a table is spread, the host will precede his guests, in company with one of the ladies, followed by the hostess. The gentlemen present will conduct the other ladies in like manner.

When no table is set, the refreshments will be handed around, and the guests will help themselves. At intervals iced beverages will be passed around the rooms for the refreshment of the guests. White or very light-colored kid gloves are worn during the evening, except at supper.

DINNERS.

Invitations to dinner parties may be sent out

from two days to a fortnight before the appointed time. They should be in the name of the lady, and the acceptance or declination should be sent immediately, addressed to her. It is also necessary that the lady should be informed if any guest, after accepting the invitation, will be prevented by subsequent circumstances from attending. The invitations should specify the hour of dining, and the guests should be punctual in arriving. In Washington, the hour for dinner parties is from four to seven o'clock. When dinner is announced, each gentleman should offer his left arm to a lady, if the dining room is on the same floor; but if they are to descend the stairs, the lady should be on the wall side. The host should lead the way, and the lady should follow the company, on the arm of a gentleman of the party. She will, of course, take the head of the table, and should have a gentleman on either hand to assist her in carving. Her husband should sit opposite her, with a lady on each side of him. These positions next to the host and hostess are considered the places of honor. Soup will constitute the first course, which must be noiselessly sipped from the side of the spoon. It is impolite to ask for a second plate. Fish usually follows soup. It is helped with a silver knife, and eaten with a silver fork, assisted by a piece of bread held in the left hand. A knife of the usual metal is deemed highly injurious to the flavor of fish. After this course, meat, fowls, &c., are served. The napkins are to be unfolded and spread upon the knees. Finger glasses will be brought on with the dessert. They contain warm water with a bit of lemon in it. It is usual to dip a corner of the napkin in the water, and wipe the lips; also to dip the fingers in, and wipe them on the napkin. It is highly disgusting to spit or blow the nose with a loud explosive noise at table. The knife is never used to convey food to the mouth; the fork being generally sufficient for the purpose; or it may be assisted by a piece of bread in the left hand. The servants should each be furnished with a clean white napkin, with which to handle the plates of the guests. Clean white gloves are sometimes used. Servants should never be ordered, but always requested to perform their duties. The host and his lady should betray no vexation if anything goes wrong in the arrangement, or seem to notice it, if possible to avoid doing so. Ladies must be helped first. It is not necessary to wait until all are helped before beginning to eat. Wine is not drunk until the second course is over. The ladies are helped to the kind of wine they prefer by the gentleman next to them. When the ladies retire, the gentlemen should rise with them, and stand until they leave the dining-room. Coffee may be served either in the dining-room or parlor.

DEPORTMENT IN THE STREET.

The toilet should be thoroughly adjusted before leaving the house, even to the putting on the gloves. The great point in walking is to be natural. All affected airs are contemptible. On the other hand, an awkward or slovenly gait should not be mistaken for a natural one.

A gentleman meeting a lady acquaintance should wait to be recognized by her, and should raise his hat while bowing to her. Also, in meeting a gentleman of your acquaintance who is accompanied by a lady, you should raise your hat out of respect to her, and he should respond in like manner to your salutation. If a gentleman salutes the lady you accompany, you should return it, if she recognizes it. It is not necessary to take off the glove in shaking hands with a lady, neither should the gentleman make the advance. In walking, the gentleman should keep next to the carriage way.

A gentleman should never omit a punctilious observance of the rules of politeness to his recognized acquaintances, from an apprehension that he will not be met with reciprocal marks of respect. For instance, he should not refuse to raise his hat to an acquaintance who is accompanied by a lady, lest her escort should, from ignorance or stolidity, return his polite salutation with a nod of the head.

It is better not to see him, than to set the example of a rude and indecorous salutation. In all such cases, and in all cases, he who is most courteous has the advantage, and should never feel that he has made a humiliating sacrifice of his personal dignity. It is for the party whose behavior has been boorish to have a consciousness of inferiority.

A gentleman meeting a lady acquaintance on the street, should not presume to join her in her walk without ascertaining that his company would be entirely agreeable. It might be otherwise, and she should frankly say so. A married lady usually leans upon the arm of her husband; but single ladies do not, in the day, take the arm of a gentleman, unless they are willing to acknowledge an engagement. Gentlemen always give place to ladies, and to gentlemen accompanying ladies, in crossing the street.

BALLS.

Balls to which anybody who chooses may go, and take whom he pleases, by buying a ticket, are avoided by many ladies, and with good reason. But select balls, under judicious and responsible management, are not liable to this objection. In such cases the ladies are invited, and none others go. The gentleman who accompanies a lady will dance the first set with her. She may then dance with other gentlemen. At a private party a gentleman may offer to dance with a lady without an introduction, but at balls the rule is different. The gentleman should respectfully offer his arm to the lady who consents to dance with him, and lead her to her place. At the conclusion of the set he will conduct her to a seat, offer her any attention, or converse with her. A gentleman should not dance with his wife, and not too often with the lady to whom he is engaged.

VISITS TO OFFICIAL PERSONS ON BUSINESS.

Calls upon the Cabinet and other administrative officers in Washington, upon official business, should be made during business hours, at their respective offices. The visitor should be provided with a card, which the messenger will deliver. He should briefly state his business, and remain not a moment longer than necessary. Members of Congress may be seen at their lodgings, or at the Capitol while the Houses are in session. Very little ceremony is necessary if the visitor be an influential constituent.

THE PRESIDENT.

The President has a grand levee on the first of January, when people crowd to the Executive

Mansion, in such numbers, that of late years, it has been found necessary to shut the doors, and only admit as many at one time as can be conveniently accommodated with space within. After this opening levee, which occurs in the morning, the President has periodical levees on a certain evening of each week, or, since Mr. Buchanan's term commenced, every fortnight. These are also well attended. The public are admitted indiscriminately on these occasions, but no refreshments are offered. The Marshal for the District introduces the public. The President has also a sort of weekly summer levee in the south grounds, in which the performance of the Marine Band is the principal attraction.

The President is accessible to private individuals who desire to see him on business, and he has also set apart an hour or two on certain days in each week for receiving the friendly visits of the public. These regulations are often varied, and we therefore refrain from giving them. The President never accepts invitations to dine, or makes social visits. An invitation to dine with the President is accepted, notwithstanding a previous engagement. It is proper to address him as *Mr. President*.

On New Year's day the New York custom prevails in Washington of keeping open house. Not only the President and Cabinet, but many other gentlemen, official and private, have adopted it, and furnish their voluntary guests with refreshments.

We have thus given the leading rules and principles of Washington Etiquette. To supply all the details of ceremony in social and official life would require a volume, and compel us to depart from the plan which we had marked out for ourselves.

IMPORTANT TO STRANGERS!!

MORRISONS' VIEWS

OF THE

PUBLIC BUILDINGS

AND

STATUES

OF

WASHINGTON CITY.

THIS COLLECTION CONSISTS OF

25 SUPERIOR STEEL ENGRAVINGS,

EMBRACING

EVERYTHING OF INTEREST TO A STRANGER,

With a description of the same, neatly put up in a gilt case, which can be found at any of our bookstores.

This work no Stranger should be without.

W. H. & O. H. MORRISON,

Publishers, Booksellers, and Stationers,

No. 440 Pennsylvania Avenue,

WASHINGTON CITY.

STATIONERY in every variety and style, Wholesale and Retail.

BLANK BOOKS of all kinds and sizes, from the smallest pass-book to the largest used in the counting house. Blank-books made to order at the shortest notice.

MISCELLANEOUS BOOKS in every department of literature and science. Books ordered and imported from every part of the world at the shortest notice.

SCHOOL BOOKS on hand at all times, consisting of such as are in general use in our city and surrounding country.

LAW BOOKS. Special attention is paid to this department of our business, consisting of a full and general assortment of all published, and in all cases of the last and best editions. Reports and Statutes of all the States furnished at the shortest notice. Liberal discounts are made to regular purchasers, or when large orders are made.

CONGRESSIONAL DOCUMENTS on hand in large collections, some of which are very scarce and hard to be obtained. Persons in want of such, by sending us their orders will be sure of getting them if they are to be obtained under any circumstances.

www.ingramcontent.com/pod-product-compliance
Lightning Source LLC
Chambersburg PA
CBHW022229010526
44113CB00033B/779